Contents

BIRDLAND

— JOSEF ZAWINUL

D.S. TO [A] (TAKE REPEATS)
PLAY THROUGH [C] (TAKE REPEATS)
GO TO [E] (TAKE REPEAT), THEN TAKE ⊕

BOLIVIA

— CEDAR WALTON

CHAMELEON

(MED. FUNK)

C VERSION

- HERBIE HANCOCK/
PAUL JACKSON/
HARVEY MASON/BENNIE MAUPIN

INTRO

(BASS) N.C.

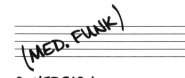

BASS CONT. SIM.

PLAY 3x

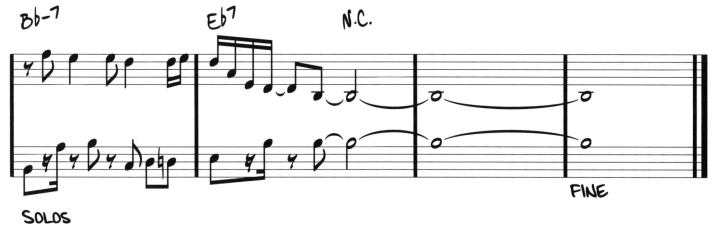

FINE

SOLOS

AFTER SOLOS, D.S. AL FINE
(TAKE REPEATS)

500 MILES HIGH

(MED. LATIN)

C VERSION

— CHICK COREA/NEVILLE POTTER

AFTER SOLOS, D.S. AL ⊕
(PLAY PICKUP) (NO REPEAT)

Lucky Southern

— Keith Jarrett

(BOSSA)

C VERSION

FINE
AFTER SOLOS, D.S. AL FINE
(TAKE REPEAT)

PHASE DANCE

– PAT METHENY/ LYLE MAYS

(EVEN 8ths)

C VERSION

INTRO

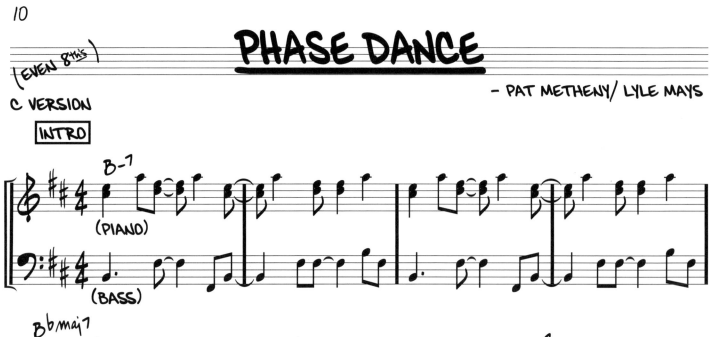

RHYTHM CONT. SIM.

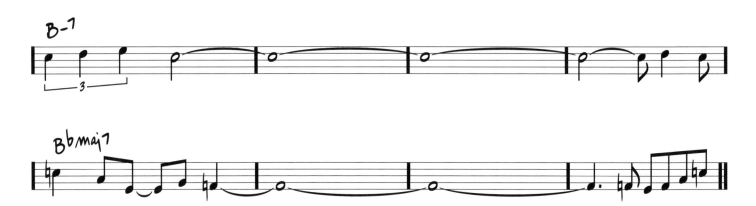

HALF-TIME FEEL

Gmaj7/A

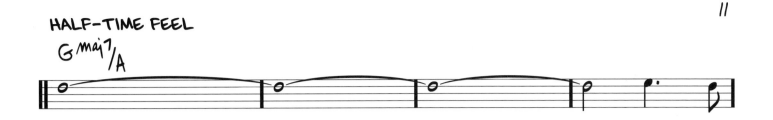

Gmaj13

END HALF-TIME FEEL

(PIANO)

B-7

BASS PLAYS INTRO

Bbmaj7

TO ⊕

AFTER SOLOS, D.S. AL ⊕
(PLAY PICKUPS)

⊕ B-7

12

Red Baron

(MED. SLOW)
MED. FUNK

— BILLY COBHAM

C VERSION

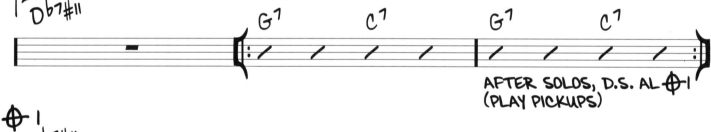

AFTER SOLOS, D.S. AL ⊕-1
(PLAY PICKUPS)

Sugar

— STANLEY TURRENTINE

C VERSION

(SWING)

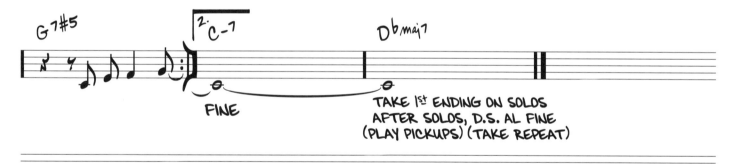

FINE

TAKE 1st ENDING ON SOLOS
AFTER SOLOS, D.S. AL FINE
(PLAY PICKUPS) (TAKE REPEAT)

RED CLAY

— FREDDIE HUBBARD

C VERSION

(STRAIGHT 8th's)

SOLOS

AFTER SOLOS, D.S. AL ⊕
(PLAY PICKUP) (TAKE REPEATS)

SPAIN

- CHICK COREA

C VERSION

(SAMBA)

F#7

E-7

A7   3   Dmaj7

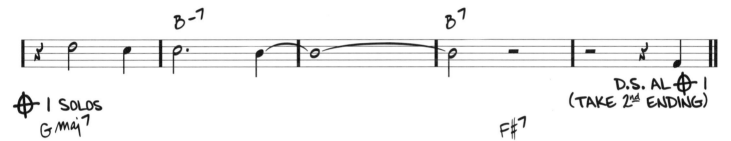

Gmaj7   C#7   F#7

B-7   B7

D.S. AL ⊕ 1
(TAKE 2nd ENDING)

⊕ 1 SOLOS
Gmaj7   F#7

(1st X ONLY) - - - - - ⌐

E-7   A7

Dmaj7   Gmaj7   C#7

F#7   B-7   B7

(LAST X)
AFTER SOLOS, D.S. AL ⊕ 2

⊕ 2
G6/9   Bbmaj7#5   B-11   E7sus4

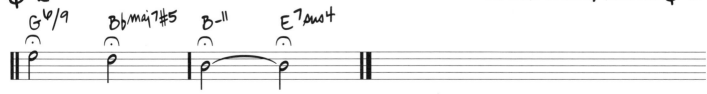

Birdland

- Josef Zawinul

Bb VERSION

CHAMELEON

(MED. FUNK)

Bb Version

- HERBIE HANCOCK/
PAUL JACKSON/
HARVEY MASON/BENNIE MAUPIN

INTRO

(BASS) N.C.

BASS CONT. SIM.

PLAY 3X

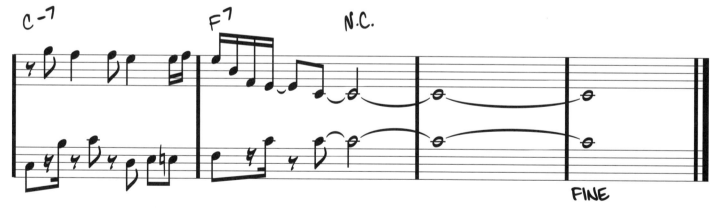

FINE

SOLOS

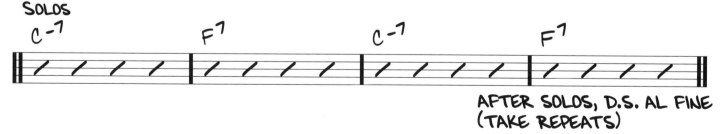

AFTER SOLOS, D.S. AL FINE
(TAKE REPEATS)

500 Miles High

- CHICK COREA/NEVILLE POTTER

Lucky Southern

(BOSSA)

— KEITH JARRETT

Bb Version

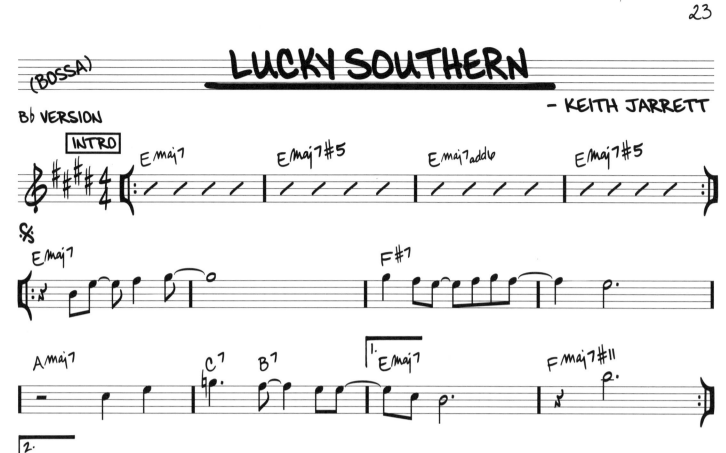

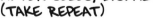

FINE
AFTER SOLOS, D.S. AL FINE
(TAKE REPEAT)

24

PHASE DANCE

— PAT METHENY / LYLE MAYS

(EVEN 8ths)

Bb VERSION

INTRO

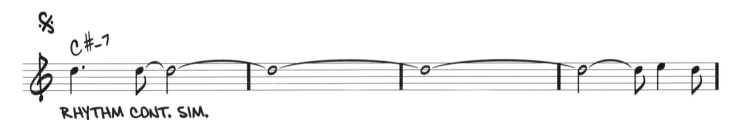

RHYTHM CONT. SIM.

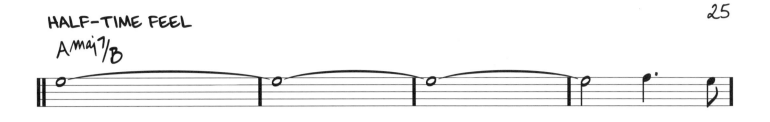

HALF-TIME FEEL

END HALF-TIME FEEL

(PIANO)

BASS PLAYS INTRO

TO

AFTER SOLOS, D.S. AL
(PLAY PICKUPS)

RED BARON

- BILLY COBHAM

Bb VERSION

AFTER SOLOS, D.S. AL ⊕-1
(PLAY PICKUPS)

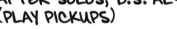

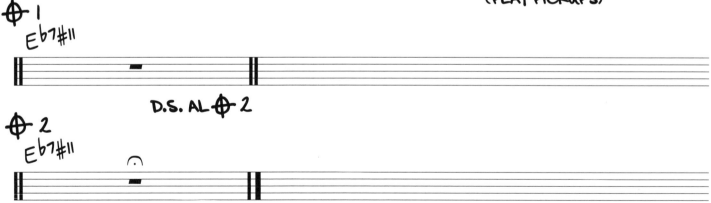

Sugar

— STANLEY TURRENTINE

(SWING)

Bb VERSION

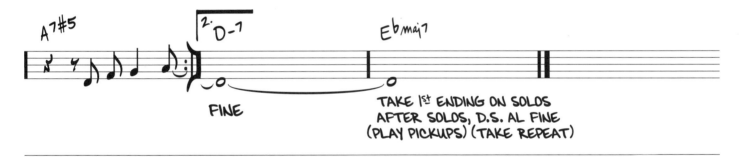

FINE

TAKE 1st ENDING ON SOLOS
AFTER SOLOS, D.S. AL FINE
(PLAY PICKUPS) (TAKE REPEAT)

Red Clay

- FREDDIE HUBBARD

Bb VERSION

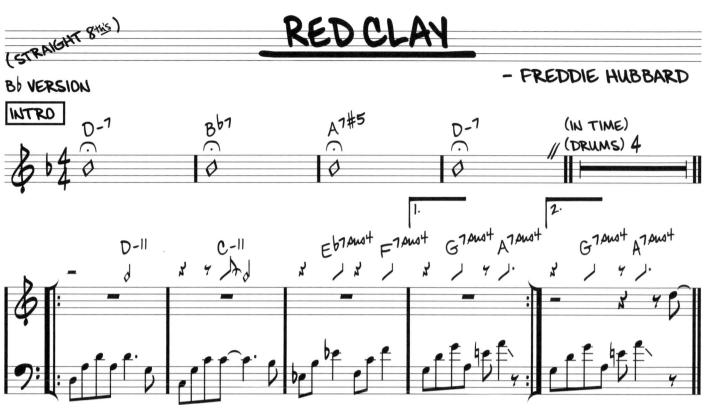

SOLOS

AFTER SOLOS, D.S. AL ⊕
(PLAY PICKUP) (TAKE REPEATS)

SPAIN

- CHICK COREA

Bb VERSION

D.S. AL ⊕ 1
(TAKE 2nd ENDING)

⊕ 1 SOLOS

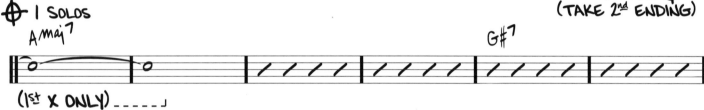

(1st X ONLY)

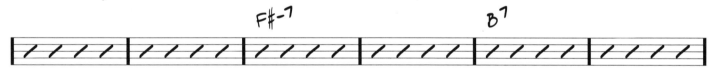

(LAST X)
AFTER SOLOS, D.S. AL ⊕ 2

⊕ 2

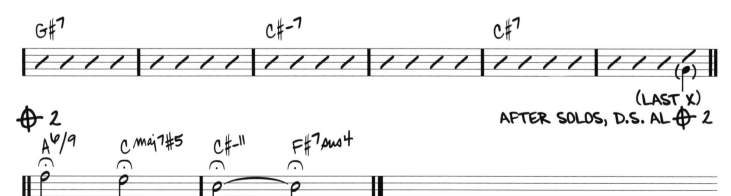

BIRDLAND

— JOSEF ZAWINUL

Eb VERSION

(BASS & PIANO)

** (1ST X ONLY)

*** AFTER D.S.,
PLAY UPSTEM PICKUP
AND CONTINUE AT E

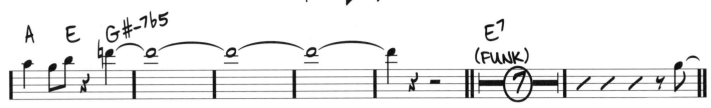

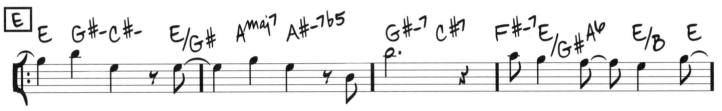

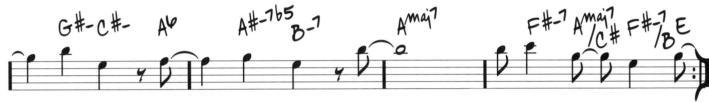

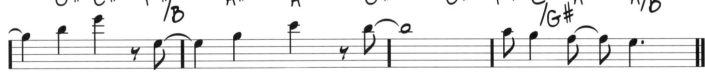

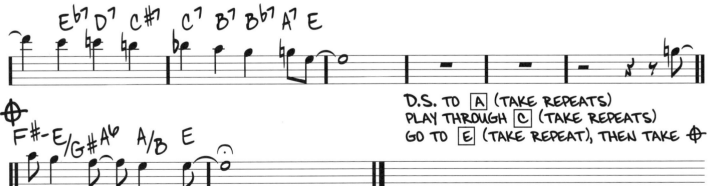

D.S. TO A (TAKE REPEATS)
PLAY THROUGH C (TAKE REPEATS)
GO TO E (TAKE REPEAT), THEN TAKE ⊕

BOLIVIA

– CEDAR WALTON

CHAMELEON

(MED. FUNK)

Eb VERSION

– HERBIE HANCOCK/
PAUL JACKSON/
HARVEY MASON/BENNIE MAUPIN

INTRO

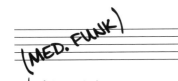

(BASS) N.C.

BASS CONT. SIM.

PLAY 3X

FINE

SOLOS
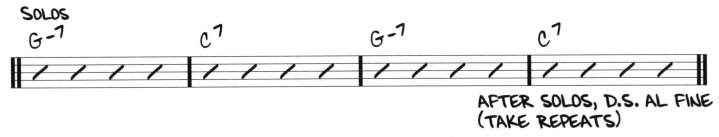

AFTER SOLOS, D.S. AL FINE
(TAKE REPEATS)

500 MILES HIGH

(MED. LATIN)

Eb VERSION

— CHICK COREA/NEVILLE POTTER

AFTER SOLOS, D.S. AL ⊕
(PLAY PICKUP) (NO REPEAT)

Lucky Southern

— Keith Jarrett

Eb Version

(BOSSA)

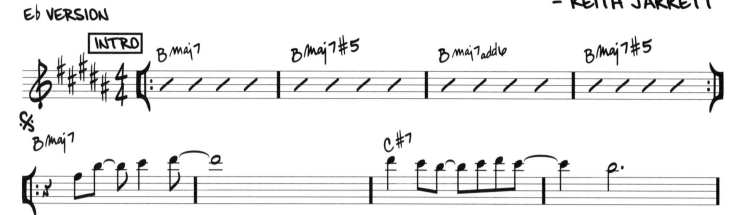

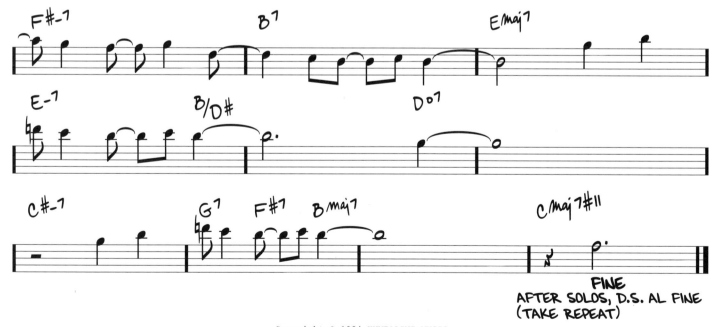

FINE
AFTER SOLOS, D.S. AL FINE
(TAKE REPEAT)

Phase Dance

– PAT METHENY/ LYLE MAYS

(EVEN 8th's)

Eb Version

RHYTHM CONT. SIM.

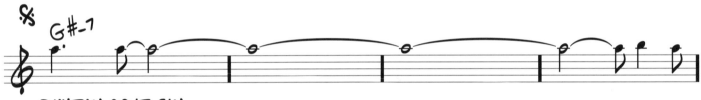

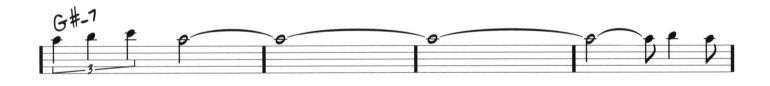

HALF-TIME FEEL
E maj7/F#

E maj13
END HALF-TIME FEEL

(PIANO)

G#-7

BASS PLAYS INTRO

G maj7
TO ⊕

AFTER SOLOS, D.S. AL ⊕
(PLAY PICKUPS)

⊕ G#-7

Red Baron

— BILLY COBHAM

Eb VERSION

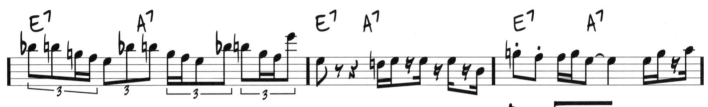

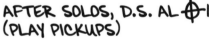

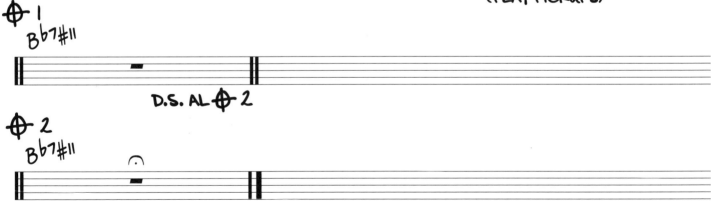

Sugar

— STANLEY TURRENTINE

(SWING)

Eb Version

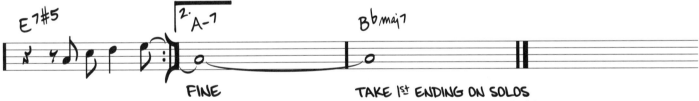

FINE

TAKE 1st ENDING ON SOLOS
AFTER SOLOS, D.S. AL FINE
(PLAY PICKUPS) (TAKE REPEAT)

RED CLAY

— FREDDIE HUBBARD

(STRAIGHT 8ths)

Eb VERSION

INTRO

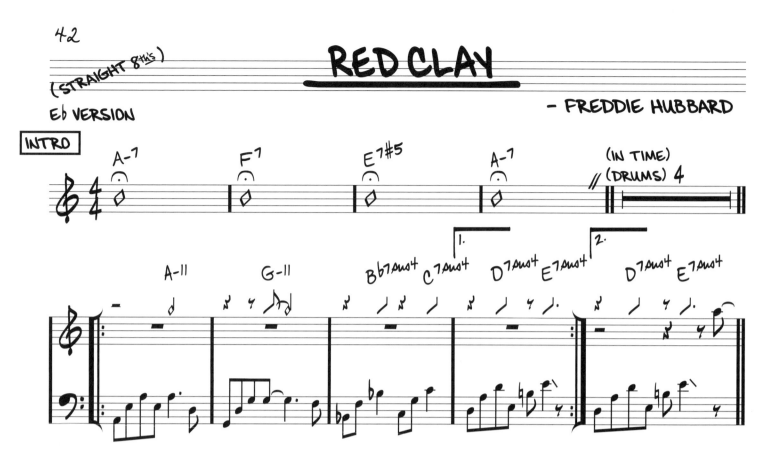

SOLOS

AFTER SOLOS, D.S. AL ⊕
(PLAY PICKUP) (TAKE REPEATS)

SPAIN

– CHICK COREA

(SAMBA)

Eb VERSION

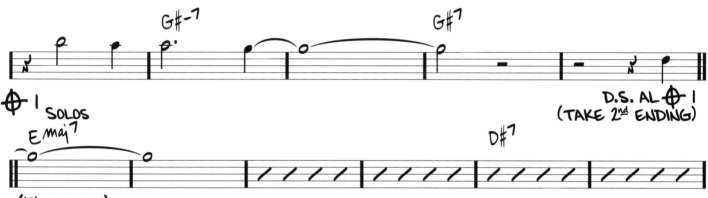

D.S. AL ⊕ 1
(TAKE 2nd ENDING)

(1st X ONLY)

(LAST X)
AFTER SOLOS, D.S. AL ⊕ 2

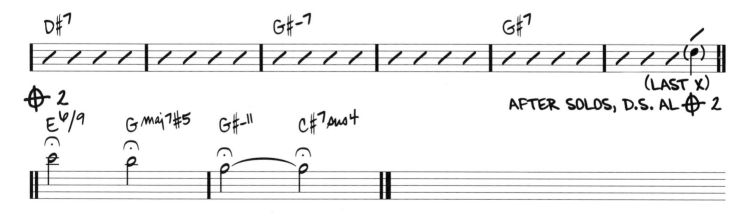

BIRDLAND

– JOSEF ZAWINUL

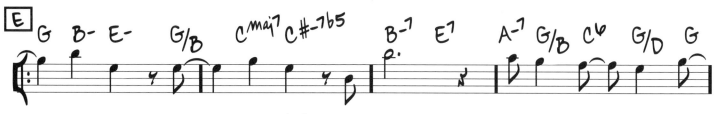

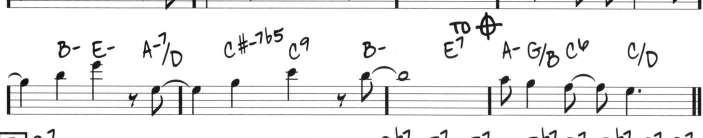

D.S. TO [A] (TAKE REPEATS)
PLAY THROUGH [C] (TAKE REPEATS)
GO TO [E] (TAKE REPEAT), THEN TAKE ⊕

BOLIVIA

— CEDAR WALTON

REPEAT HEAD IN/OUT (TAKE REPEATS)
D.C. FOR SOLOS (TAKE REPEATS)
AFTER SOLOS, D.C. AL ⊕

CHAMELEON

(MED. FUNK)

9: C VERSION

- HERBIE HANCOCK/
PAUL JACKSON/
HARVEY MASON/BENNIE MAUPIN

INTRO

(BASS)   N.C.

BASS CONT. SIM.

PLAY 3x

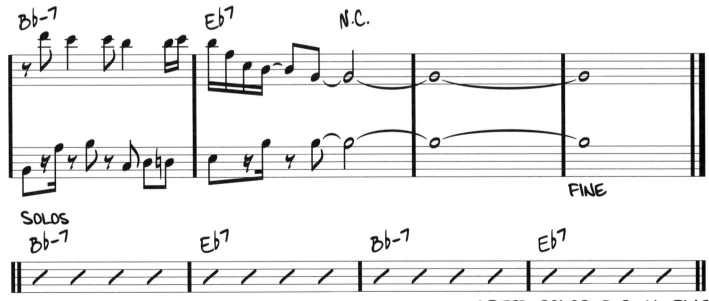

FINE

SOLOS
Bb-7   Eb7   Bb-7   Eb7

AFTER SOLOS, D.S. AL FINE
(TAKE REPEATS)

500 MILES HIGH

- CHICK COREA/NEVILLE POTTER

50

Lucky Southern

– KEITH JARRETT

(BOSSA)

𝄢 C VERSION

INTRO | Dmaj7 | Dmaj7#5 | Dmaj7add6 | Dmaj7#5 |

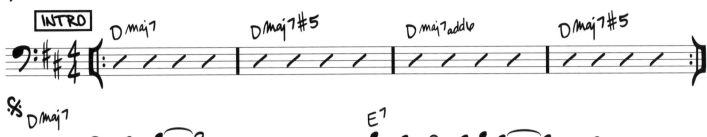

Dmaj7 .... E7

Gmaj7 .... Bb7 A7 1. Dmaj7 .... Ebmaj7#11

2. Dmaj7 .... F#-7

E-7 .... F#-7

A-7 .... D7 .... Gmaj7

G-7 .... D/F# Fo7

E-7 .... Bb7 A7 Dmaj7 .... Ebmaj7#11

FINE
AFTER SOLOS, D.S. AL FINE
(TAKE REPEAT)

PHASE DANCE

– PAT METHENY/ LYLE MAYS

(EVEN 8ths)

𝄢 C VERSION

INTRO

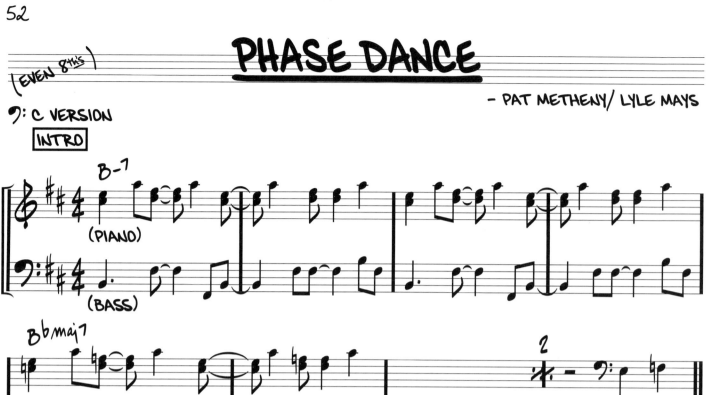

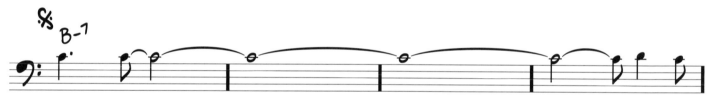

RHYTHM CONT. SIM.

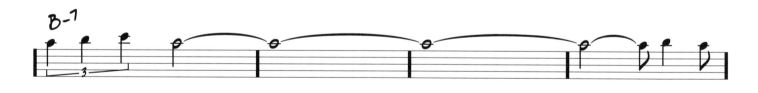

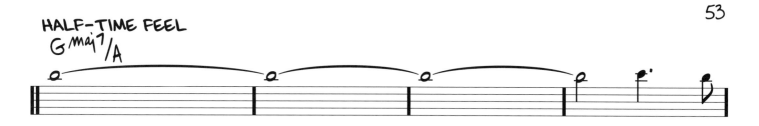

HALF-TIME FEEL
Gmaj7/A

Gmaj13   END HALF-TIME FEEL

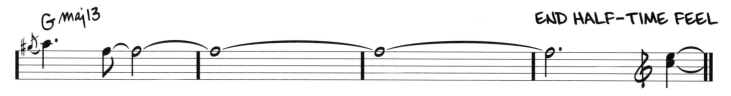

(PIANO)

B-7

BASS PLAYS INTRO

Bbmaj7

TO ⊕

AFTER SOLOS, D.S. AL ⊕
(PLAY PICKUPS)

⊕ B-7

Red Baron

- BILLY COBHAM

Sugar

— STANLEY TURRENTINE

(SWING)

𝄢: C VERSION

FINE

TAKE 1st ENDING ON SOLOS
AFTER SOLOS, D.S. AL FINE
(PLAY PICKUPS) (TAKE REPEAT)

RED CLAY

— FREDDIE HUBBARD

(STRAIGHT 8ths)

🎵: C VERSION

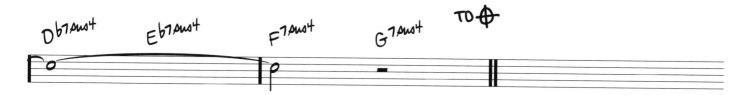

SOLOS

AFTER SOLOS, D.S. AL ⊕
(PLAY PICKUP) (TAKE REPEATS)

SPAIN

- CHICK COREA

9: C VERSION

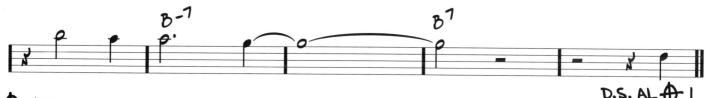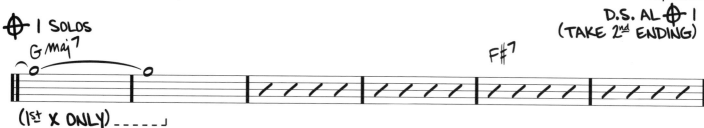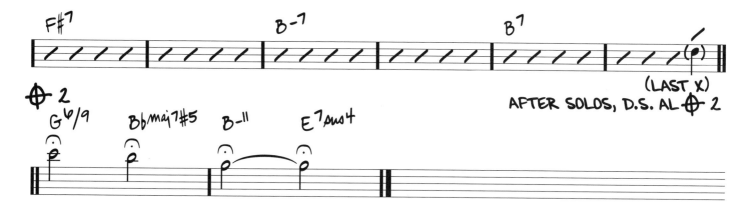

59

THE REAL BOOK MULTI-TRACKS

TODAY'S BEST WAY TO PRACTICE JAZZ!
Accurate, easy-to-read lead sheets and professional, customizable audio tracks accessed online for 10 songs

1. MAIDEN VOYAGE PLAY-ALONG

Autumn Leaves • Blue Bossa • Doxy • Footprints • Maiden Voyage • Now's the Time • On Green Dolphin Street • Satin Doll • Summertime • Tune Up.
00196616 Book with Online Media...........$17.99

2. MILES DAVIS PLAY-ALONG

Blue in Green • Boplicity (Be Bop Lives) • Four • Freddie Freeloader • Milestones • Nardis • Seven Steps to Heaven • So What • Solar • Walkin'.
00196798 Book with Online Media...........$17.99

3. ALL BLUES PLAY-ALONG

All Blues • Back at the Chicken Shack • Billie's Bounce (Bill's Bounce) • Birk's Works • Blues by Five • C-Jam Blues • Mr. P.C. • One for Daddy-O • Reunion Blues • Turnaround.
00196692 Book with Online Media...........$17.99

4. CHARLIE PARKER PLAY-ALONG

Anthropology • Blues for Alice • Confirmation • Donna Lee • K.C. Blues • Moose the Mooche • My Little Suede Shoes • Ornithology • Scrapple from the Apple • Yardbird Suite.
00196799 Book with Online Media...........$17.99

5. JAZZ FUNK PLAY-ALONG

Alligator Bogaloo • The Chicken • Cissy Strut • Cold Duck Time • Comin' Home Baby • Mercy, Mercy, Mercy • Put It Where You Want It • Sidewinder • Tom Cat • Watermelon Man.
00196728 Book with Online Media...........$17.99

6. SONNY ROLLINS PLAY-ALONG

Airegin • Blue Seven • Doxy • Duke of Iron • Oleo • Pent up House • St. Thomas • Sonnymoon for Two • Strode Rode • Tenor Madness.
00218264 Book with Online Media........$17.99

7. THELONIOUS MONK PLAY-ALONG

Bemsha Swing • Blue Monk • Bright Mississippi • Green Chimneys • Monk's Dream • Reflections • Rhythm-a-ning • 'Round Midnight • Straight No Chaser • Ugly Beauty.
00232768 Book with Online Media........$17.99

8. BEBOP ERA PLAY-ALONG

Au Privave • Boneology • Bouncing with Bud • Dexterity • Groovin' High • Half Nelson • In Walked Bud • Lady Bird • Move • Witches Pit.
00196728 Book with Online Media..........$17.99

9. CHRISTMAS CLASSICS PLAY-ALONG

Blue Christmas • Christmas Time Is Here • Frosty the Snow Man • Have Yourself a Merry Little Christmas • I'll Be Home for Christmas • My Favorite Things • Santa Claus Is Comin' to Town • Silver Bells • White Christmas • Winter Wonderland.
00236808 Book with Online Media..........$17.99

10. CHRISTMAS SONGS PLAY-ALONG

Away in a Manger • The First Noel • Go, Tell It on the Mountain • Hark! the Herald Angels Sing • Jingle Bells • Joy to the World • O Come, All Ye Faithful • O Holy Night • Up on the Housetop • We Wish You a Merry Christmas.
00236809 Book with Online Media..........$17.99

11. JOHN COLTRANE PLAY-ALONG

Blue Train (Blue Trane) • Central Park West • Cousin Mary • Giant Steps • Impressions • Lazy Bird • Moment's Notice • My Favorite Things • Naima (Niema) • Syeeda's Song Flute.
00275624 Book with Online Media........$17.99

12. 1950S JAZZ PLAY-ALONG

Con Alma • Django • Doodlin' • In Your Own Sweet Way • Jeru • Jordu • Killer Joe • Lullaby of Birdland • Night Train • Waltz for Debby.
00275647 Book with Online Media........$17.99

13. 1960S JAZZ PLAY-ALONG

Ceora • Dat Dere • Dolphin Dance • Equinox • Jeannine • Recorda Me • Stolen Moments • Tom Thumb • Up Jumped Spring • Windows.
00275651 Book with Online Media........$17.99

14. 1970S JAZZ PLAY-ALONG

Birdland • Bolivia • Chameleon • 500 Miles High • Lucky Southern • Phase Dance • Red Baron • Red Clay • Spain • Sugar.
00275652 Book with Online Media........$17.99

15. CHRISTMAS TUNES PLAY-ALONG

The Christmas Song (Chestnuts Roasting on an Open Fire) • Do You Hear What I Hear • Feliz Navidad • Here Comes Santa Claus (Right down Santa Claus Lane) • A Holly Jolly Christmas • Let It Snow! Let It Snow! Let It Snow! • The Little Drummer Boy • The Most Wonderful Time of the Year • Rudolph the Red-Nosed Reindeer • Sleigh Ride.
00278073 Book with Online Media........$17.99

The Best-Selling Jazz Book of All Time Is Now Legal!

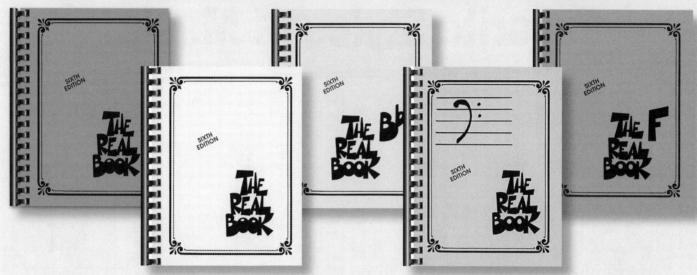

The Real Books are the most popular jazz books of all time. Since the 1970s, musicians have trusted these volumes to get them through every gig, night after night. The problem is that the books were illegally produced and distributed, without any regard to copyright law, or royalties paid to the composers who created these musical masterpieces.

Hal Leonard is very proud to present the first legitimate and legal editions of these books ever produced. You won't even notice the difference, other than all the notorious errors being fixed: the covers and typeface look the same, the song lists are nearly identical, and the price for our edition is even cheaper than the originals!

VOLUME 1

00240221	C Edition	$39.99
00240224	B♭ Edition	$39.99
00240225	E♭ Edition	$39.99
00240226	Bass Clef Edition	$39.99
00286389	F Edition	$39.99
00240292	C Edition 6 x 9	$35.00
00240339	B♭ Edition 6 x 9	$35.00
00147792	Bass Clef Edition 6 x 9	$35.00
00451087	C Edition on CD-ROM	$29.99
00200984	Online Backing Tracks: Selections	$45.00
00110604	Book/USB Flash Drive Backing Tracks Pack	$79.99
00110599	USB Flash Drive Only	$50.00

VOLUME 2

00240222	C Edition	$39.99
00240227	B♭ Edition	$39.99
00240228	E♭ Edition	$39.99
00240229	Bass Clef Edition	$39.99
00240293	C Edition 6 x 9	$35.00
00125900	B♭ Edition 6 x 9	$35.00
00451088	C Edition on CD-ROM	$30.99
00125900	The Real Book – Mini Edition	$35.00
00204126	Backing Tracks on USB Flash Drive	$50.00
00204131	C Edition – USB Flash Drive Pack	$79.99

VOLUME 3

00240233	C Edition	$39.99
00240284	B♭ Edition	$39.99
00240285	E♭ Edition	$39.99
00240286	Bass Clef Edition	$39.99
00240338	C Edition 6 x 9	$35.00
00451089	C Edition on CD-ROM	$29.99

VOLUME 4

00240296	C Edition	$39.99
00103348	B♭ Edition	$39.99
00103349	E♭ Edition	$39.99
00103350	Bass Clef Edition	$39.99

VOLUME 5

00240349	C Edition	$39.99
00175278	B♭ Edition	$39.99
00175279	E♭ Edition	$39.99

VOLUME 6

00240534	C Edition	$39.99
00223637	E♭ Edition	$39.99

Also available:

00151290	The Real Book – Enhanced Chords	$29.99
00282973	The Reharmonized Real Book	$39.99

HAL•LEONARD®

Complete song lists online at www.halleonard.com

Prices, content, and availability subject to change without notice.

REAL BOOKS
Now Available in Your Favorite Styles of Music!

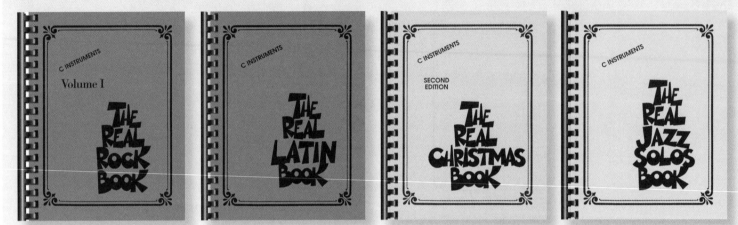

The Real Books are the best-selling jazz books of all time. Since the 1970s, musicians have trusted these volumes to get them through every gig, night after night. The problem is that the books were illegally produced and distributed, without any regard to copyright law, or royalties paid to the composers who created these musical masterpieces. Hal Leonard is very proud to present the first legitimate and legal editions of these books ever produced – and now has also published brand new volumes with a blockbuster selection of songs in a variety of genres.

Also available:

00295069	The Real Bebop Book Eb Edition	$34.99
00154230	The Real Bebop Book C Edition	$34.99
00295068	The Real Bebop Book Bb Edition	$34.99
00240264	The Real Blues Book	$34.99
00310910	The Real Bluegrass Book	$35.00
00240223	The Real Broadway Book	$35.00
00125426	The Real Country Book	$39.99
00240355	The Real Dixieland Book C Edition	$32.50
00122335	The Real Dixieland Book Bb Edition	$35.00
00294853	The Real Dixieland Book Eb Edition	$35.00
00240268	The Real Jazz Solos Book	$30.00
00240348	The Real Latin Book C Edition	$37.50
00127107	The Real Latin Book Bb Edition	$35.00
00118324	The Real Pop Book – Vol. 1	$35.00
00295066	The Real Pop Book Vol. 1 Bb Edition	$35.00
00286451	The Real Pop Book - Vol. 2	$35.00
00240437	The Real R&B Book C Edition	$39.99
00276590	The Real R&B Book Bb Edition	$39.99
00240313	The Real Rock Book	$35.00
00240323	The Real Rock Book – Vol. 2	$35.00
00240359	The Real Tab Book	$32.50
00240317	The Real Worship Book	$29.99

THE REAL CHRISTMAS BOOK

00240306	C Edition	$35.00
00240345	Bb Edition	$32.50
00240346	Eb Edition	$35.00
00240347	Bass Clef Edition	$35.00
00240431	A-G CD Backing Tracks	$24.99
00240432	H-M CD Backing Tracks	$24.99
00240433	N-Y CD Backing Tracks	$24.99

HAL•LEONARD®
Complete song lists online at
www.halleonard.com

Prices, content, and availability subject to change without notice.

REAL BOOKS
Featuring Your Favorite Artists!

The Real Books are the best-selling jazz books of all time. Since the 1970s, musicians have trusted these volumes to get them through every gig, night after night. The problem is that the books were illegally produced and distributed, without any regard to copyright law, or royalties paid to the composers who created these musical masterpieces. Hal Leonard is very proud to present the first legitimate and legal editions of these books ever produced – and now has also published brand new volumes paying homage to some of the greatest artists of all time.

00295714	**The Beatles Real Book**	$29.99
00240440	**The Trane Book**	$22.99
00269721	**The Miles Davis Real Book** C Edition	$24.99
00269723	**The Miles Davis Book** Bb Edition	$24.99
00240235	**The Duke Ellington Real Book**	$22.99
00120809	**The Pat Metheny Real Book** C Edition	$27.50
00252119	**The Pat Metheny Real Book** Bb Edition	$24.99
00240358	**The Charlie Parker Real Book** C Edition	$19.99
00275997	**The Charlie Parker Real Book** Eb Edition	$19.99
00240331	**The Bud Powell Real Book**	$19.99

Complete song lists online at www.halleonard.com

Prices, content, and availability subject to change without notice.